REMAKING THE
JOHN

THE INVENTION AND REINVENTION OF THE TOILET

for spiffing up my work over the years.

Thanks from "Francie"

Twenty-First Century Books
A division of Lerner Publishing Group, Inc.
241 First Avenue North
Minneapolis, MN 55401 USA

For reading levels and more information, look up this title at www.lernerbooks.com.

Main body text set in Gamma ITC Std 11/15.
Typeface provided by International Typeface Corp.

CONTENTS

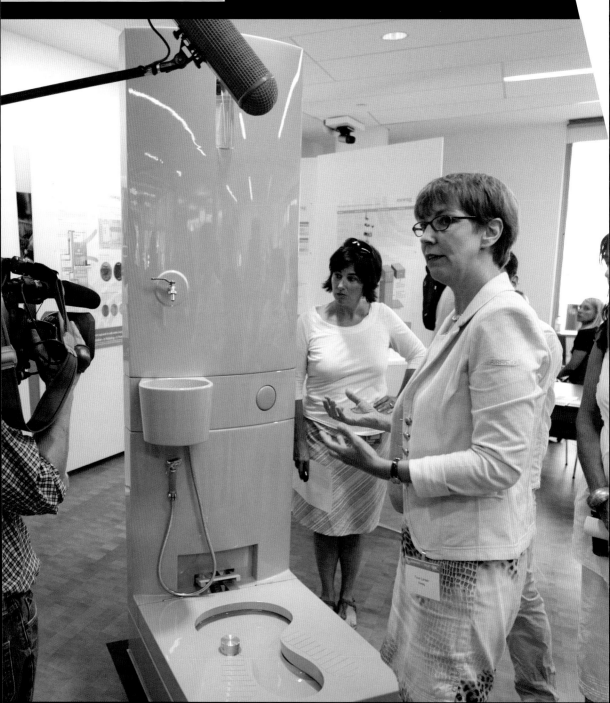

> ## The art of living together without turning the city into a dunghill has [to be] repeatedly discovered.
>
> —Aldous Huxley, twentieth-century British writer and social commentator, n.d.

Half a solid pound (0.2 kilograms), plus 47 ounces (1.4 liters) of liquid. According to the medical journal *Gut*, that's how much feces and urine an adult human produces, on average, every day. It adds up to about 182 pounds (83 kg) of feces and 134 gallons (507 liters) of urine per person per year. Multiply that by seven or eight billion—as the number of people on Earth steadily increases—and you've got a lot of waste.

What should be done with it? People have only a few options: leave it, bury it, put it in waterways, or recycle it as fertilizer or fuel. Inventions along one or another of these lines turn up over and over again throughout history. From the citizens of the world's first settlements to astronauts living on the International Space Station (ISS), humans have figured out various ways to dispose of body wastes. Sometimes the ideas have been brilliant, and sometimes they've led to terrible suffering. Toilet history includes everything from the hunt for the cause of infectious disease to marvels of engineering. Toilet habits even turn up in religion, literature, and art. There are centuries of creative responses to the question "What should we do with all this waste?"

Facing page: *At the annual Reinvent the Toilet Fair, sponsored by the Bill and Melinda Gates Foundation, inventors present toilets that use little water, kill germs, recycle waste, and are affordable for people living in poor nations.*

CHAPTER ONE

PITS, POTS, AND PIPES

Outside the camp you shall have a place set aside to be used as a latrine. You shall also keep a trowel in your equipment and with it, when you go outside to ease nature, you shall first dig a hole and afterward cover up your excrement.

—*The Book of Deuteronomy*

The great outdoors has always been the number one place for people to "do their business." More than ten thousand years ago, before the invention of farming, people practiced open defecation. Early hunter-gatherers urinated and defecated in waterways or on the ground. Since hunter-gatherer bands moved regularly, they never had to deal with the long-term accumulation of waste in one spot.

When people began to farm, they settled into small villages. Over time, agriculture began to support larger communities. Villages became large towns. Early city dwellers used rivers, lakes, or simple holes in the ground as toilets. They also used pots and other containers. When the containers were full, people dumped the waste in nearby waterways.

Because townspeople didn't move regularly the way hunter-gatherers did, they had to figure out how to dispose of accumulating waste. Early farmers learned that human and animal waste can enrich the soil. Some farmers collected human waste, allowed it to decompose, and then spread it on their fields. The decayed waste released nutrients that helped plants grow taller and stronger.

But human waste also contains germs and parasites. Archaeologists (scientists who study past cultures) have found

Facing page: *This structure in the ancient ruins of Mohenjo Daro in modern-day Pakistan was probably a toilet. In addition to toilets, the city had a network of sewers that emptied into the Indus River.*

evidence of parasites in the organs of ancient mummies and in other ancient human remains. The parasites probably spread to humans who ate food or drank water that was contaminated with human waste.

Even though ancient peoples didn't know about germs, they still connected the dots between filth and disease. They generally avoided drinking or eating anything that smelled or looked nasty. Ancient religious lawmakers believed that body wastes offended God. In the Hebrew Bible, the lawgiver Moses instructs the Jewish people to keep their camps clean. He tells them to dig holes to use as toilets and to cover their waste with dirt. Such religious laws protected public health, even if that wasn't the lawmakers' intention.

INDOOR PLUMBING

About five thousand years ago, the villagers of Skara Brae in present-day Scotland constructed what might be the world's first indoor toilets. Archaeologists have found closet-like openings in the walls of the village's ancient stone cottages. The openings had drains beneath them. Historians think it's likely that these areas served as toilets.

Some houses in the ancient city of Mohenjo Daro (built in what is now Pakistan around 2600 BCE) also had indoor drains. They were connected to large covered sewers that ran along the city's main streets. The sewers were made of clay and brick and carried wastewater to the Indus River.

In ancient times, the best toilets were reserved for the upper classes. For example, the royal inhabitants of a palace in the ancient Greek city of Knossos used a water-washed toilet almost four thousand years ago. After

This ceramic chamber pot from ancient China dates to the third or fourth century CE. Designed specifically for men, the vessel has an opening for urination and a handle for emptying the waste.

each use, a servant would dump a bucket of water to flush out the toilet bowl. The contents emptied into a clay sewer pipe, and because the palace was on a hill, the pipe emptied downhill.

The Roman Empire, which flourished from 27 BCE to 476 CE, was based in Rome, Italy. At its height, it stretched from Britain to the Middle East. Engineers built sewers and toilets in cities throughout the empire. At its largest, the population of Rome came close to one million. The city had 144 public restrooms. Privacy wasn't a concern. The typical public toilet had ten to twenty seats, with no walls between them. People sat next to one another on long benches with keyhole-shaped openings. A channel of running water underneath the seats carried away the waste.

When Roman citizens were about town, they could relieve themselves at public toilets such as this one. People sat close together, with no partitions between the seats. Ancient Romans weren't modest when it came to using the toilet.

The waste emptied into a system of sewers that flowed into the Maxima Cloaca, which means "greatest sewer" in Latin. Built around 600 BCE, this sewer drained into Rome's Tiber River. The Romans believed in an active spirit world, and they even worshipped a goddess of sewers named Cloacina. She protected sewers and sewer workers.

At home, Romans used pots and pails as toilets. They dumped the contents into gutters outside their houses, into nearby cesspits (underground holding tanks), or out the window onto the street below. In about 200 CE, the Roman legal official Ulpian offered advice for those hit by waste thrown from an apartment window. He wrote, "If the apartment is divided among several tenants, redress [compensation] can be sought only against that one of them who lives in that part of the apartment from the level of which the liquid has been poured. The same will hold good if the vessel or the liquid has been thrown from a balcony."

In 97 CE, Sextus Julius Frontinus became the water commissioner of Rome. He set strict rules forbidding Romans to dump wastes into public water supplies. He wrote, "No one shall with malice pollute the waters where they issue publicly. Should anyone pollute them, his fine shall be ten thousand sesterti [ancient Roman coins, equal to about $500 in modern times]."

Frontinus also wrote a booklet called *On the Water-Management of the City of Rome*. In it, he noted that public policies regarding wastewater had cleaned up the city's foul-smelling air. Romans believed that this dirty air, which they called miasma, caused disease. Frontinus also painstakingly listed all the city's thousands of water pipes.

The writer Martial supplied many witty observations about Roman life. In one of his writings, a snobbish dinner host comments, "It's a fine dinner." One of the guests replies, "Very fine, I confess, but tomorrow it will be nothing, or rather today, or rather a moment from now it will be nothing; a matter for . . . a crock by the roadside to take care of." The "crock by the roadside" that Martial mentioned was like an ancient porta-potty. The container would have been set out on the road by a fuller (a maker of woolen cloth). Fullers collected human urine and let

it sit until it turned to ammonia, which they used to clean and bleach sheep's wool. Romans used stale urine to whiten their teeth too.

I SEE LONDON

In the first few centuries of the Common Era, London was part of the Roman Empire. Engineers from Rome built a Roman-style sewer system in the city. In the early 400s CE, the Roman Empire started to decline in power. The Romans pulled out of London, and its sewer system fell into ruins. Fast-forward nine hundred years to the 1300s. By then London was home to about eighty thousand people. Yet, even with a large population like this, public toilets were rare. When they were out and about, Londoners simply relieved themselves in alleys or waterways. At home, they used containers called chamber pots.

Some royalty and other wealthy Londoners owned silver and gold chamber pots, but most chamber pots were made of clay or metal. The pots had narrow necks to prevent waste from splashing back up from inside the pot. Most homes had no room set aside for toilet use. Instead, families moved chamber pots from room to room and relieved themselves as needed. They kept pots by the bed for nighttime use and in the dining room for use after meals—with little concern for privacy. Residents dumped the contents into cesspits or simply into the street.

Peveril Castle, built in the 1100s in Derbyshire, England, was equipped with a garderobe. Users sat at a toilet inside, located beneath the small window (center), and waste fell through the chute underneath the window (center, bottom), to the yard outside.

Some people emptied their own chamber pots, and some had servants empty the pots.

In the Tower of London and in other British castles, little cubicles called garderobes served as toilet rooms. (The ammonia smell of old urine was said to "guard robes"—or protect clothing—from fleas.) Garderobes extended outward from the exterior walls of the castle. They had holes in the floor through which waste dropped directly to the ground below. At some castles, servants dumped the contents of chamber pots into the moats (defensive waterways) that surrounded the castles.

Monasteries were some of the most sanitary places in Europe during the Middle Ages (about 500 to 1500). There, toilet rooms were built over streams, so waste dropped directly into running water, which carried it away. The toilet room in a monastery was called a reredorter because it was at the rear of the dorter, or dormitory.

In farming areas and other sparsely populated places of Europe, people dumped waste into brick- or stone-lined cesspits. They also built outhouses, or small sheds placed above pits in the ground. Inside outhouses, a user would sit on a bench with a hole directly over the pit. When the pits beneath outhouses got full, people covered them with dirt and moved the structure to a new pit. Sometimes people planted trees on the old site. Trees grew well in the rich soil. Cesspits had to be emptied or they would overflow. Sometimes farmers bought the waste from cesspits to use for fertilizer. Other times the waste was dumped in waterways or just piled somewhere far from the house.

NIGHT SOIL

In most European cities, cesspits were not cleaned regularly. Waste often seeped out of them. It rotted in the streets and trickled into wells and rivers. At the same time, animals of all varieties lived in cities alongside humans. Horses provided transportation. Cows, pigs, and poultry provided food. Dogs and cats served as companions to humans. "Street soil" in medieval cities was a sticky mix of garbage of all sorts. It included human and animal manure, dead dogs and cats, and ashes from fireplaces.

In London, workers gathered muck from streets and cesspits and sold it to farmers. By law, these workers had to carry out their smelly, unsightly duties at night. These "night-soil men" descended into cesspits on ropes. They gathered sludge in buckets and hauled it on carts to nearby farms.

If a city had sewers—and most didn't—they were usually open gutters. Their main function was to channel rainwater rather than human waste. London had many open gutters, and city records are full of complaints about people contaminating them with human waste. For example, court records dated August 9, 1314, tell us that Alice Wade "made a wooden pipe connecting the seat of the privy [toilet] in her solar [private room] with the gutter, which is frequently stopped up by the filth therefrom . . . and the neighbours under whose houses the gutter runs are greatly inconvenienced by the stench." Judges ruled that Wade had to remove the pipe within forty days. In 1310 John le Luter complained that his neighbor's cesspit was too close to his property, "so that his house is inundated and his [dirt] wall rotted by the sewage." The court ordered that both parties pay to clean the cesspit and to build a stone wall to replace the dirt wall.

Rats and other rodents fed on the filth of a city's human and animal waste. Fleas lived in the rats' fur, and some fleas carried the deadly disease bubonic plague. An outbreak of the plague known as the Black Death killed millions of people throughout Europe and the Middle East in the 1300s.

During the Black Death in Europe, doctors wore bird-head hoods. The beak was filled with strong-smelling herbs and spices, supposed to combat miasma, which was thought to cause disease. In actuality, plague spread via flea bites, and fleas lived in the fur of rats and other rodents. These animals abounded in London and other big cities, where they fed on human waste and other garbage sitting in the streets.

At the time, no one knew how the plague and other diseases spread. People blamed miasma. Town and city leaders sought to sweep up their streets to get rid of the stink. After Europe recovered from the Black Death, cities continued to grow. And so did their waste.

CHAPTER TWO

OVERFLOW!

Let no one, whoever he may be, before, at, or after meals, early or late, foul the staircases, corridors, or closets with urine or other filth, but go to suitable, prescribed places for such relief.

—*European handbook on manners, late sixteenth century*

By the 1500s, large European cities were filthy. The Dutch scholar Erasmus, writing in 1530, expressed disgust at the straw-strewn floor of a British house he visited: "The floors are made of clay, and covered with marsh rushes, constantly piled on one another, so that the bottom layer remains sometimes for twenty years, incubating spittle, vomit, the urine of dogs and men, the dregs of beer, the remains of fish, and other nameless filth."

Local governments passed laws about keeping streets clean but rarely enforced them. Cities had no boards of health or sanitation, and residents were careless about cleanliness. European artists Pieter Brueghel the Elder in the 1500s and Rembrandt in the 1600s painted men squatting outside to defecate and women lifting their skirts to urinate on the ground. (Women of this era didn't wear underpants.)

A NEW TOILET

Hoping to clean things up, inventors devised better toilet systems. In the 1500s, chamber pots got an upgrade. European furniture makers designed chairs with boxes underneath to hold chamber pots. Hinged box lids concealed the pots. These toilet chairs were

Facing page: *This British woodcut, printed in* A Book of Roxburghe Ballads *in the 1800s, shows the filth of sixteenth-century London. A woman defecates in the road, another woman pours waste from a second-story window, children play near an open sewer, and animals feed on human waste.*

known variously as close stools, necessary stools, conveniences, and night commodes. Some were very fancy, made with carved wood and plush fabrics.

In the 1590s, British writer John Harington invented the first mechanical flush toilet. It had a tank full of water that sat above a toilet bowl. A system of handles, levers, and weights triggered the tank to release its water to flush the bowl. The water drained into a pipe that ran into an underground cesspit.

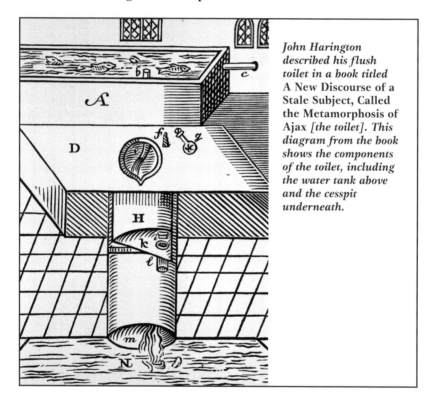

John Harington described his flush toilet in a book titled A New Discourse of a Stale Subject, Called the Metamorphosis of Ajax *[the toilet]. This diagram from the book shows the components of the toilet, including the water tank above and the cesspit underneath.*

Harington's godmother, Elizabeth I (1533–1603), was the queen of England at the time. She ordered a flush toilet from him and reportedly liked it. But she was almost the only one. The toilet didn't catch on with the public partly because its straight drainpipe allowed foul—and flammable—sewer gas to waft up into the room where the toilet sat.

JOHN, JAKE, AND MORE

John Harington called his toilet the Ajax, a variation on "the jake" or "Jake's house," other English slang terms for toilets. In Harington's era, Jake was a nickname for a crude country person. Going to Jake's house or to the jake was a funny way to talk about going to the privy. "Going to the john" became common slang for going to the toilet in the United States. Other names for toilets of this era were water closets (for toilets that flushed with water) and earth closets (for toilets in which the contents were covered with dirt).

The most common nickname for the toilet in modern Britain is the loo. It may have its origins in the French phrase *gardez l'eau* (watch out for water), pronounced "gardy loo" in Britain. This is the warning people yelled during the Middle Ages before they emptied their chamber pots out the window. The word *toilet* comes from the French word *toilette*, meaning a "little cloth." It originally referred to the general act of grooming, not just to going to the bathroom. *Lavatory* comes from the Latin verb *lavare*, meaning "to wash."

NEW WORLD . . . SAME TOILETS

In the 1500s and the 1600s, Europeans began to colonize North America. British attempts to settle Jamestown, Virginia, began in failure. In the winter of 1609–1610, most colonists in the settlement's fort died of starvation and disease, including typhoid fever.

Typhoid is spread by the fecal-oral route. That is, a person gets sick by swallowing even a tiny speck of feces from an infected person. In Jamestown, dirty water, food, and hands were responsible for the spread of typhoid, but colonists didn't know that. They continued to believe the miasma theory, blaming bad odors for illness. To fight miasma, survivors of Jamestown's deadly winter made laws to improve their air. One law required residents to walk 450 yards (411 meters) outside the fort to "do the necessities." The law further said:

> Nor shall any one aforesaid, within lesse then a quarter of
> one mile [0.4 kilometer] from the Pallizadoes [the palisades,

or fort walls], dare to doe the necessities of nature, since by these unmanly, slothfull, and loathsome immodesties, the whole Fort may bee choaked, and poisoned with ill aires, and so corrupt.

In 1620 British pilgrims sailed on the *Mayflower* to New England. The 102 passengers lived in crowded conditions below deck for sixty-six days. They relieved themselves in chamber pots. About fifty men made up the ship's crew. They relieved themselves at the head, or the front, of the ship. (To this day, a ship's toilet is called the head.) Sailors sat over holes cut through the ship's planks or hung their bottoms over the edge of the ship. The unraveled end of a rope provided wiping material.

Pilgrims and other European settlers brought the methods of waste disposal they had known in Europe to their new American homes. For this reason, sanitation in the American colonies was no better than in Europe. Town wells supplied much of the drinking water in towns and other settlements. Disease-laden fluids from cesspits often seeped into wells, infecting Americans with waterborne diseases such as typhoid. Even so, with fewer people, colonial towns were usually healthier than the more crowded European cities of the time.

Chamber pots of various kinds, the open outdoors, and outhouses were familiar and reliable options for toilet facilities. Colonists called the outhouse the privy or the necessary. (*Privy* is from the Latin word *privatus*, meaning "private.") But visiting the outhouse wasn't necessarily private. In Williamsburg, Virginia, archaeologists have unearthed many five- and even seven-seaters, with no walls between the seats.

Colonial American cities did not have effective sewer systems, and colonists dumped raw sewage anywhere that was convenient. Scientists of the era didn't fully understand disease transmission, though they saw a connection between illness and dirt. So, faced with outbreaks of yellow fever (spread by mosquitoes), smallpox (spread by an airborne virus), and typhoid (spread by a waterborne bacterium), city officials tried to promote cleanliness. In 1744 the city council in New

This elegantly crafted mahogany toilet chair was used in colonial New York around 1775. The seat once had comfortable upholstery, and the owner would have placed a chamber pot beneath it to catch waste.

York passed a law for "Cleansing the Streets, Lanes and Alleys." It required homeowners to "Rake and Sweep together all the Dirt, Filth and Soil lying in the Street" into piles every Friday. The city council hired men to remove the piles of "Carrion [dead animals], Guts, Garbiage, Oyster shells, Dunghills [piles of excrement], Ashes, Dirt, Soil and Filth" to be "thrown into the River, or some other convenient Place." Citizens paid a fine for not sweeping. The fine climbed for anyone dumping their "Close Stools, or Pots of Ordure [excrement] and Nastiness" into the street instead of the river. The public paid little attention to the laws.

A PATRIOTIC CONCERN

Sanitary rules tightened, at least in the military, when American colonists began fighting for their independence from Great Britain. At the start of the Revolutionary War (1775–1783), dysentery (severe and sometimes deadly diarrhea) and other diseases were rampant in the army. To manage human waste, officers ordered soldiers to dig trenches at the edge of camps, use them as toilets, and cover the contents with dirt every day. "The Health of an army principally Depends upon Cleanness," army headquarters declared.

Officers put harsh measures into place to persuade men to use the sanitary trenches. Guards were to "make prisoner of any Soldier who shall attempt to ease himself at any where; but at the proper necessary [toilet] and five lashes [with a whip] are to be immediately order'd." But most soldiers were farmers. They came from small communities where they relieved themselves in the woods and fields or used communal toilets with people they knew. Uncomfortable using smelly, open trenches with strangers, they defied the rule, faced punishment, and relieved themselves in and around the camp instead. In a private letter, army commander-in-chief George Washington expressed disgust at the toilet habits of many of his troops. "They are an exceeding dirty & nasty people," he wrote.

After the war, the new nation's first census showed that less than 4 percent of the population lived in cities. With 42,520 residents, Philadelphia, Pennsylvania, was the largest city in the United States in 1790. That year the city's water had "become so corrupt by the multitude of sinks [cesspits] and other receptacles of impurity as to be almost unfit to be drank." Inventor and statesman Benjamin Franklin remodeled his Philadelphia house at this time. He had a brick-lined, circular cesspit built in the yard. A pipe carried waste from Franklin's privy to the pit.

Boston, Massachusetts, with a population of 18,320, formed a board of health in 1799. Famous for his Revolutionary midnight ride warning patriots of a British attack, Paul Revere was the board's first president. Under his leadership, the board decreed on October 2, 1799, "that as the season has now arrived when the emptying of the contents of privies will be the least offensive to the inhabitants [because smells are reduced in cold weather], it be earnestly recommended to and required of the inhabitants, immediately to empty all Privies whose contents are within 18 inches [46 centimeters] of the surface."

THE S-PIPE

On the other side of the Atlantic, Europeans continued to look for solutions to the problems of poor sanitation. In 1775 Scottish watchmaker Alexander Cummings perfected John Harington's flush toilet by bending its outflow pipe into an S shape. The bend prevented sewer gases such as methane from wafting back into the toilet room. This eliminated both bad smells and the risk of explosions.

By the early 1800s, the improved flush toilet was all the rage. Companies that made pottery and tableware also produced toilet bowls in large numbers. Soon toilets were installed all over London and other European and US cities too.

In the United States of the early 1800s, large numbers of new immigrants swelled the population of New York City to a quarter million. The flushing toilet was a hit with these city dwellers, but cesspits and sewers couldn't hold the huge increase in wastewater that resulted. Especially when it rained, cesspits overflowed into the streets. Sewage ran into cellar apartments, where one in every twenty-five New Yorkers lived. New York and other cities were soon filthier than ever as raw sewage overflowed into streets, cellars, and waterways.

A SICKLY SEASON

Meanwhile, the Industrial Revolution had transformed Great Britain. People flooded into British cities from small towns and rural communities to work in factories. By the early 1800s, the population of London had reached 1.5 million. The city didn't have adequate plumbing or housing for this many people. Serious overcrowding plus poor sanitation was a deadly combination.

British author Jane Austen remarked on the risk to public health through the mouth of a character in her novel *Emma* (1815). Emma's father, Mr. Woodhouse, is convinced that "in London it is always a sickly season. Nobody is healthy in London, nobody can be." Expressing an enduring belief in the miasma theory, he adds, "The air is so bad!"

Mr. Woodhouse was a fussbudget, but he was not all that wrong. This description from an 1850 edition of the *Edinburgh Review* in

PLUCKING A ROSE

British women who lived during Jane Austen's lifetime (1775–1817) used the phrase "plucking a rose" to mean going to the toilet. In British villages, the toilet was usually in the garden, which might contain roses, so "plucking a rose" was polite code for excusing oneself to the garden.

When they were away from home, wealthy British women carried a cunning invention called a bourdaloue. Designed for females, a bourdaloue was a narrow china bowl. It looked like a gravy boat (the dish that holds Thanksgiving turkey gravy). Some bourdaloues were quite beautiful, with floral patterns and real gold trim. Women tucked them up under their long skirts and held them between their thighs when they needed to urinate during long carriage rides, at dances, or at other public gatherings. (According to legend, they were named for French preacher Louis Bourdaloue, who gave fascinating but extra-long sermons in church. Women in the congregation didn't want to miss a word, so they kept the containers with them to relieve themselves during services.) Since women didn't yet wear underpants, the devices were easy to put into place and easy to remove. Servants had the job of emptying them.

When away from home, wealthy women relieved themselves into bourdaloues, which could be tucked up under a woman's skirts and between the thighs.

Scotland summed up the condition of many crowded British and US cities:

> The offensive refuse which even animals will bury out of
> sight, is brought into perpetual contact with human beings. It
> stagnates in the courts and alleys, flows into the cellars, and is
> sucked up into the walls. Men, women and children eat, drink
> and sleep, surrounded by its disgusting effluvia [discharge].
> The pig in its sty is not more familiar with its own odor.

In London, the River Thames provided residents with much of
their drinking water. But the river ran thick and black with raw sewage,
garbage, and industrial wastes. Bacteria thrived in the dirty water.
Conditions were perfect to welcome a new disease: cholera.

CHAPTER THREE

THE DARK STREAM
OF DISEASE

> We live in muck and filthe. We aint got no privez [toilets],
> no dust bins, no drains, no water splies [supplies], and no
> drain or suer [sewer] in the whole place. . . . The Stenche of
> a Gully-hole is disgustin. We al of us suffur, and numbers are
> ill, and if the Colera comes Lord help us.
>
> —Times *(London), letter to the editor, sent by fifty-four London slum dwellers, 1849*

Late on the night of Monday, June 26, 1832, an Irish immigrant in New York City named Fitzgerald came home violently ill. Still in extreme pain the next morning, he sent for a doctor. The doctor could do nothing to help, but Fitzgerald began to feel better on his own. The two Fitzgerald children, however, suddenly came down with agonizing stomach cramps. They vomited and emitted gallons of fishy-smelling diarrhea. Their skin shriveled and turned blue. They gasped for air. The Fitzgerald children were dead in a day. Their mother died that Friday. Cholera had arrived in New York City.

THE FIRST WAVE

Like typhoid, cholera spreads through feces-infested water. In the early 1830s, Americans tracked the disease's progress in the newspapers as it spread across Asia, Europe, and then the Atlantic Ocean. With railroads, canal boats, trade ships, and other fast-moving conveyances of the era, cholera traveled quickly. No one knew what caused it or how to stop it. New York City officials tried to protect the city by forbidding ships to dock within 300 yards (274 m) of shore.

Cholera strikes fast, and people were terrified of the disease. One New Yorker reported going out in the morning feeling well and later in the day falling down in the street, "as if knocked down with an axe." The *New York Evening Post* reported, "To

Facing page: *In this 1858 illustration from the British magazine* Punch, *the filthy River Thames is shown as a bearer of death. Raw sewage flowed into the river from gutters and cesspits. People didn't know that the sewage transmitted cholera, but they knew that the dirty river water was making them sick.*

see individuals well in the morning & buried before night, retiring apparently well & dead in the morning is something which is appalling to the boldest heart."

Within days after the cholera outbreak, New York, Boston, and other cities began to clean up months'—even decades'—worth of stinky street soil. Scientists still thought the smell itself carried disease. Workers shoveled up human excrement, decaying dead animals, and rotting garbage. Removing the stinking matter was a good idea. But it was often just dumped off piers, where it infected waters. Cholera killed more than one hundred New Yorkers a day.

That summer of 1832, cholera traveled west with the army battalion of US general Winfield Scott. He assembled a group of 950 soldiers on the East Coast just as cholera was breaking out there. Their orders were to fight Native Americans in Wisconsin and Illinois during the Black Hawk War (1832). Scott's unit traveled by steamboat across the Great Lakes. At each stop, soldiers sick and dying of cholera were left behind. By the time troops reached Chicago, Illinois, only 350 soldiers were fit to fight.

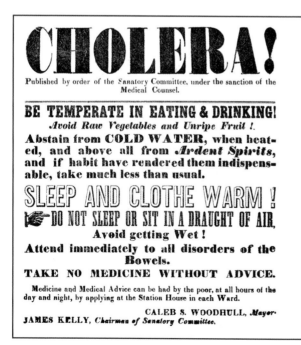

CHOLERA!

Published by order of the Sanatory Committee, under the sanction of the Medical Counsel.

BE TEMPERATE IN EATING & DRINKING!
Avoid Raw Vegetables and Unripe Fruit !.
Abstain from COLD WATER, when heated, and above all from *Ardent Spirits*, and if habit have rendered them indispensable, take much less than usual.

SLEEP AND CLOTHE WARM !
☞**DO NOT SLEEP OR SIT IN A DRAUGHT OF AIR,**
Avoid getting Wet !
Attend immediately to all disorders of the Bowels.
TAKE NO MEDICINE WITHOUT ADVICE.

Medicine and Medical Advice can be had by the poor, at all hours of the day and night, by applying at the Station House in each Ward.

CALEB S. WOODHULL, *Mayor.*
JAMES KELLY, *Chairman of Sanatory Committee.*

In 1849 the New York Sanitary Committee posted warnings about cholera, but the advice was of little help. Doctors then didn't know that the disease spread through water that had been infected with human waste.

PIGS AND SNOW

The dramatic death toll of cholera spurred hundreds of cities to form local boards of health to protect the public from disease. But sanitation measures in the United States and Europe were still inadequate. Many places had no street cleaners except for free-roaming animals, which survived by eating excrement and garbage. British writer Charles Dickens wrote about the street pigs of New York City when he visited in 1842. He described the bright colors of parasols and women's clothes as he set out to cross Broadway. Then he warned,

> Take care of the pigs. Two portly sows are trotting up behind this carriage, and a select party of half-a-dozen gentlemen hogs have just now turned the corner. . . . They are the city scavengers, these pigs. Ugly brutes they are. . . . They are never attended upon, or fed, or driven, or caught, but are thrown upon their own resources in early life.

In the 1840s, cholera returned to Europe. Scientists still didn't know how it spread, and most blamed foul-smelling air. In London, British doctor John Snow worked like a detective to discover cholera's causes. By carefully mapping a cluster of severe cholera cases in 1848, he realized deaths had occurred in households that drew water from a pump on Broad Street. He studied the water and saw white flecks in it. These were remnants of the watery, milky diarrhea of cholera victims. They had seeped in from a basement cesspit only 3 feet (1 m) away from the pump's underground well. A person didn't catch cholera by breathing bad air, Snow realized, but by swallowing water contaminated with feces. Snow wrote a letter to the *Medical Times and Gazette* describing his next steps: "I had an interview with the Board of Guardians of St. James's parish. . . . In consequence of what I said, the handle of the pump was removed on the following day."

Removing the pump handle seemed to work. Snow continued, "In two or three days after the use of the water was discontinued the number of fresh attacks became very few." The case of the Broad Street pump handle would become famous in the history of science, but at the time, hardly anyone paid attention to Snow's discovery. Most scientists stuck to the miasma theory.

Cholera was back in the United States in 1849. President James Polk had recently left office. He visited New Orleans, Louisiana, even though he was already in poor health and knew the city to be "in a cholera atmosphere." Afterward, he complained of "a derangement of stomach & bowels." Polk died a few weeks later.

THE GREAT STINK

John Snow died in 1858, his work on cholera mostly ignored. But no one in London that unusually hot summer could ignore the horrendous smell of the River Thames. It was so horrific that Londoners referred to the stench as the Great Stink. Some members of the British government, which normally met in buildings near the river, fled town.

London's inadequate sewers and street drains emptied into the Thames. The river ran thick with raw sewage, garbage, and the effluvia of factories. Dr. William Budd had read Snow's studies on infectious disease and carried on his work. Regarding the Great Stink, Budd observed:

> For the first time in the history of man, the sewage of nearly three millions of people had been brought to seethe and ferment under a burning sun, in one vast open cloaca [sewer] lying in their midst. The result we all know. Stench so foul, we may well believe, had never before ascended to pollute this lower air. Never before, at least, had a stink risen to the height of a historic event.

The British government realized it had to take action. Joseph Bazalgette rose to the challenge. As chief engineer for London's Metropolitan Commission of Sewers, he proposed constructing a massive sewer system. The costly project would require 318 million bricks and would take two decades to complete. This 82-mile (132 km) sewer superhighway would run alongside the Thames, catching runoff from drains that had previously flowed directly into the river. Using gravity and a series of pumping stations, the system would move sewage out of the city and discharge it back in the river nearer the sea.

Designing and constructing the London sewer was one of the great engineering feats of the nineteenth century. Bazalgette wrote that his plan was simple in theory but that putting it into action "certainly was a very troublesome job. We would sometimes spend weeks in drawing up plans and then suddenly come across some railway or canal [blocking the sewer's route] that upset everything, and we had to begin all over again."

THE SANITARY REVOLUTION

Great Britain's sanitary revolution spread to the United States. Sewers didn't just make cities tidier and less smelly, scientists and politicians realized, but they were actually necessary for public health.

Public health reformer Lemuel Shattuck of Boston researched and wrote the hugely influential *Report of the Sanitary Commission of Massachusetts 1850*. In it Shattuck wrote, "The dark stream of disease and death, is every day and every hour crowded with victims, carried down upon its ever flowing current beyond the limits of time." Shattuck called for setting up public health boards across the country. He wrote

Workers lay sewer pipe in West Philadelphia in 1883. The creation of sewage systems in Philadelphia and other big cities led to improved sanitation and less disease.

that each board should include "a Superintendent of Common Drains and Sewers, to superintend the location and construction of these important aids to comfort and health."

A few years later, in 1854, cholera killed 6 percent of Chicago's 112,000 residents. An article in the *Chicago Daily Tribune* of that year insisted that something be done to cleanse the city: "So many of the streets, the alleys, and the gutters, are ankle deep in festering corruption and rottenness; there are so many choked up drains and unmanageable sewers . . . and there is yet so much suffering and destitution among the poorer portion of our citizens and the emigrants daily arriving here."

Chicago began laying 152 miles (245 km) of underground sewers in 1859. The city's buildings and streets already sat at the level of Lake Michigan, so workers couldn't dig underground to build sewers without lake water flooding in. The only way to lay sewers was to raise the city to make room for the sewer system underneath. Workers wedged jacks under huge buildings and raised them an average of 6 feet (2 m), a method similar to jacking up a car to change a tire. The new sewer system emptied into the Chicago River, which runs through the city, and into a series of nearby canals.

Back in London, Dr. Benjamin W. Richardson, a friend of John Snow, wrote with confidence in 1877 that the proper handling of

HERE'S JOHNNY!

What's the greatest medical advance since 1840? In 2007 the *British Medical Journal* asked this question of a small group of experts and thousands of readers, mostly doctors. Respondents named hard hitters of medicine: antibiotics such as penicillin, heart transplants, and birth control pills. But toilets and sewers beat them all. The sanitary revolution won as the most important leap forward in health since 1840.

Even though big cities of the nineteenth century laid sewers underground, in many places, homes weren't connected to sewage systems. People in Europe and the United States continued to use chamber pots such as this one.

body waste was working. "With the progress of sanitary science . . . prevention will grow. Humanly-made epidemics . . . like the modern typhoid, which is fed by streams of drinking water uncleansed from human excreta [waste], such self-made epidemics will be prevented by simple mechanical skill [building sewer systems]."

Richardson was right. With toilets, better sewer systems, and improved sanitation, people became healthier and lived longer. In addition, by the end of the nineteenth century, scientists understood that germs transmitted disease. This knowledge led to even more sanitation efforts, ending cholera epidemics in Europe and the United States.

CHAPTER FOUR

MUCKING ABOUT IN THE TWENTIETH CENTURY

> Now listen, the boys in the sewer there, when we get upset we got a little motto, a little saying that gives us a little comfort in time of need. . . . "When the tides of life turn against you, and the current upsets your boat. Don't waste those tears on what might have been, just lay on your back and float."
>
> —*Ed Norton, sewer worker, played by Art Carney,* The Honeymooners, *1956*

I n the late 1800s and the early 1900s, inventors such as British plumber Thomas Crapper continued to improve the toilet. (The claim that Crapper invented the toilet is untrue. And though it's a good guess, Crapper's name is not the source of the word *crap*. It had already existed for hundreds of years before his time.) As late as 1920, however, only one in one hundred US homes had an indoor flush toilet. Outhouses were still the standard.

Outhouses were mostly wooden structures, although builders also used brick, stone, adobe (sun-baked clay), sheet metal, cardboard, and other materials. In winter, walls lined with straw, cornhusks, or bark helped keep out the cold. Pipes that ran up the back, along with cutouts carved through the doors of outhouses, provided ventilation. Usually, a crescent moon cutout marked an outhouse for women; a star or sunburst pattern meant the outhouse was for men. Fresh air helped to control odors and to diffuse the flammable gases that rose from the pits.

Outhouse pits were usually lined with wood, bricks, stones, or concrete. Most outhouses were equipped with a bucket of lime, a chemical powder that visitors sprinkled into the hole after each use. Lime kills bacteria and helps reduce odors. Some people

Facing page: Even as toilet technology improved in the twentieth century, some people still used outhouses. Traditionally, a crescent moon carved into the door designated a women's outhouse. The cutout in the door also provided ventilation.

used wood ash or plain dirt instead of lime. Farmers often spread the decomposed contents of pits onto their fields.

Joseph Gayetty had introduced toilet paper to the United States in the 1850s. He marketed his Gayetty's Medicated Paper as a health-care item, meant to cure sores and prevent swelling hemorrhoids. It was sold in tissue-paper-like packages of five hundred sheets for fifty cents, which was expensive at the time. But most American didn't want to pay for something they could get for free. They stocked their outhouses with dry natural materials, such as moss, leaves, corncobs, and even seashells. Pages from catalogs, like the thick catalogs that came free in the mail from Sears, Roebuck and Company, were a popular upgrade. Families tore the pages into squares and stuck them on a nail in the outhouse wall. Starting in 1910, the publishers of the popular magazine *Farmers' Almanac* even drilled a hole through the top corner of the magazine. That made the publication easy to hang in outhouses—both for reading and for toilet paper.

Outhouses had hundreds of nicknames. Some, such as privy, jake, Ajax, loo, convenience, head, and even garderobe, were old ones. Some, such as the White House or the Oklahoma potty, were distinct to the United States. In the 1920s, US actor Charles (Chic) Sale performed a comic routine about outhouses onstage. In 1929 he published a booklet, *The Specialist*, written in the style of his stage character, a champion privy builder named Lem Putt. Putt offers all sorts of funny—but wise—advice. Don't build your outhouse on soil that doesn't absorb moisture, he warns. "During the rainy season she's likely to be slippery." He continues:

> Take your grandpappy—goin' out there is about the only recreation he gets. He'll go out some rainy night with his nighties flappin' around his legs, and like as not when you come out in the mornin' you'll find him prone in the mud, or maybe skidded off one of them curves and wound up in the corn crib.

MODERN TIMES

In the 1920s, builders began to include bathrooms in all new houses and commercial buildings. By the late 1920s, indoor flush toilets had replaced outhouses in many areas of the United States. Americans preferred all-white toilet bowls, which looked sanitary, but mass-produced toilets and bathroom fixtures in multiple colors became available in 1927.

This advertising image from the Crane Plumbing Company shows an up-to-date residential bathroom from the United States in 1927. The white porcelain toilet looks a lot like toilets in twenty-first-century homes. The basic design hasn't changed much since the 1920s.

Restrooms—with private toilet stalls, sinks, mirrors, and separate facilities for men and women—were built in train stations, government buildings, schools, and other public places. Many men's rooms included urinals—vessels where men could stand and urinate—alongside standard toilets with seats. In some fancy restaurants and hotels, restroom attendants helped guests wash up after exiting toilet stalls. Many businesses installed pay toilets. Users had to put a coin into a slot to unlock the door of the toilet stall.

Toilet paper became common. In advertisements, manufacturers assured buyers that both doctors and plumbers recommended their toilet paper. But early toilet paper wasn't as soft and smooth as it later became. Toilet paper is made of wood pulp, and in the early days, the manufacturing process didn't remove all the tiny wood slivers. In 1935 engineers at Northern Paper mills in Green Bay, Wisconsin, solved the problem by cooking the wood pulp longer, reducing any splinters to harmless mush. Northern advertised its product as splinter-free. In the same era, a toilet paper brand called Charmin adopted a dainty logo, appearing soft and feminine to appeal to female shoppers.

In the 1930s, installing sanitary toilets and sewers became a US government undertaking. During the Great Depression (1929–1942), the global economy crashed. The administration of President Franklin Roosevelt responded by creating programs to put millions of unemployed Americans back to work.

ASK FOR BRONCO

TOILET PAPER
SUPREME QUALITY

The Most Soothing Toilet
Paper Ever Made
and the most economical

IN every roll of Bronco there are approximately 800 sheets, which is far more than in ordinary toilet rolls and nearly three times the quantity in so-called cheap rolls.

Bronco is obtainable from nearly all Stores, Stationers, Grocers, Chemists, etc.

Bronco
The De Luxe Toilet Paper

Solely Manufactured by
THE BRITISH PATENT PERFORATED PAPER Co., Ltd., LONDON, E.9
Established over 50 years; The largest makers of Toilet Rolls in the United Kingdom

A British toilet paper advertisement from the 1930s. The company boasted that its paper was a good value and softer than other brands.

The US government created posters to advertise its WPA outhouse-building campaign.

The Works Progress Administration (WPA) was the largest of these New Deal programs. The WPA hired and trained workers to build or improve public works, such as bridges and sewers. In 1938 WPA workers built a sewage treatment plant in Saint Paul, Minnesota.

In some rural areas, it wasn't practical to put in sewer lines because homes were spread too far from one another. There, WPA workers built sanitary outhouses for a small fee to improve national standards of hygiene and health. If a homeowner couldn't afford it, the outhouse was free. WPA outhouses had concrete floors and were placed in areas of naturally good drainage. Screened air vents kept out disease-spreading flies. Some outhouses even had a coat hook. The structures were graced with many new nicknames, including Roosevelt bungalows and Eleanors, after the president's wife.

But even where indoor toilets were the norm, filth remained a problem. In 1939 Anna Novak described the toilets where she worked in a meatpacking plant in Chicago. The bathrooms were so dirty "you could scrape muck off the floor with a knife." Under pressure from a labor union, the plant built two toilets for Novak's department of one hundred women. Even so, conditions were still far from ideal. Novak continued, "When we want to eat we've got to go over by the lockers and they're right on top of these two stinking toilets. If you knew the smell! And girls have to eat there! . . . You can't imagine what the combination of toilets and disinfectant and cigarette smoke and sweat and stockyards smells like!"

THE INSIDE DIRT
ON SEWAGE TREATMENT

When a toilet flushes, feces, urine, toilet paper, tampons, socks, cell phones, and whatever else ended up in the bowl washes through household plumbing pipes and into the city's sewer system. The waste joins household water from bathroom and kitchen sinks as well as water from businesses and industries.

If the city has a combined sewer system (CSS), sewer pipes also carry anything that washes into sewers from the street. That means rain, dog poop, oil and grease from cars, lawn clippings and fertilizers, pop cans, cigarette butts, and anything else that hits the ground. In a separate sewer system (SSS), street runoff flows into a different set of pipes. It usually drains, untreated, into a body of water, such as a lake.

In either system, household and business sewage flows through a maze of pipes to a treatment plant. There, a series of screens strains the sewage to remove solids such as disposable diapers and tampons, which are usually burned. Next, the sewage is directed to settling tanks. The heavier waste particles sink and form a layer of sludge. Machines called scrapers remove the sludge, and skimmers remove scum that floats to the top.

The remaining wastewater moves into aeration tanks, where underwater valves churn out thousands of air bubbles into the water. Air-loving bacteria and other microorganisms feast on the harmful waste bacteria in the water. Finally, the water is disinfected with sodium hypochlorite, the same bleach that whitens laundry. Bleach is not safe to drink, but engineers say that "dilution is the answer to pollution." In other words, small amounts of bleach in a large amount of water are not harmful.

Clean enough to drink, the water then goes back into local lakes or rivers. At this stage, it's usually cleaner than the water it joins. The sewage plant in Saint Paul, for example, releases its water into the Mississippi River. That river also supplies the city's drinking water.

Back in the sewage plant, bacteria eat away at the remaining sludge. As they digest it, they give off methane gas. Many US wastewater treatment plants capture this gas and burn it to power generators that create electricity. The plants then use the electric power.

When the bacteria have no more sludge to feed on, they die from a lack of fuel. Bacterial remains are called biosolids. Sewage treatment workers bake the biosolids at high temperatures to kill germs. Workers ship the odorless result, which looks like crumbly brownies, to farms. Though biosolids are completely sanitized at this stage, farmers rarely use this fertilizer on crops that humans eat. Farmers do use it to grow other kinds of crops, such as corn for livestock feed.

This sewage-treatment plant contains giant tanks for sanitizing solid and liquid waste. The different structures include sludge drying beds, aeration tanks, and disinfecting tanks.

FATBERG BACKUP

Sewer systems contain giant pipes that can usually accommodate all the sewage that flows through them. Occasionally, however, sewage gets stuck. In August 2013, London sewer workers needed three weeks to remove a "bus-sized fatberg" of kitchen fat mixed with disposable wipes from a sewer pipe. Sewer manager Gordon Hailwood said if the clog had not been discovered in time, "raw sewage could have started to spurt out of manholes."

GO WITH THE FLOW

After World War II (1939–1945), the US economy and population boomed. New sewer systems spread out underneath cities and rural communities across the nation.

Meanwhile, toilet technology continued to advance. Chemical toilets arrived in the 1950s. These are the toilets still used in airplanes, trains, travel trailers, and other vehicles. Since these toilets aren't connected to sewer systems, they have large holding tanks to store waste. Inside the tanks, chemicals combat germs and reduce odors. Eventually, at the end of a flight or a cross-country trip, workers pump the contents from holding tanks into a sewage system. Porta-potties became common in the 1960s. Used at construction sites and large outdoor events such as music festivals, these portable toilets also have holding-tank and chemical-disinfectant technology and must be pumped out regularly.

In the late twentieth century, industrial designers devised ways to make toilets more comfortable, more efficient, and cleaner. Some Americans replaced their standard porcelain toilet seats with padded or heated seats. To save water, cities encouraged—and sometimes required—homeowners and builders to install low-flow toilets, which use four or five times less water per flush than standard flush toilets. At airports and other large public buildings, some toilets were outfitted with motion sensors. These devices sense when someone

Bathrooms on airplanes are necessarily small and compact. The toilet contains chemical disinfectant to kill germs and reduce odors. Waste falls into a holding tank, to be emptied after the plane reaches its destination.

stands up after using the toilet, triggering the flush mechanism. Motion-sensor toilets are more sanitary than ordinary toilets because users don't have to touch germ-covered flush handles.

Meanwhile, sewage treatment plants developed better ways of filtering out germs and purifying wastewater. But sewage systems weren't foolproof. In 1993 an organism called cryptosporidium (crypto) somehow passed through the filters of a water-treatment plant in Milwaukee, Wisconsin. The city releases its treated sewage into Lake Michigan, from which is also draws its supply of drinking water. The crypto that slipped past the sewage filters sickened 400,000 people with stomach cramps and diarrhea and killed 104 people.

Such mishaps are rare. For the most part, US sewage treatment systems are extremely safe. In much of the world, sanitary toilets and sewage systems have reduced disease and improved health. Partly because of sewers and indoor toilets, average human life expectancy on Earth increased from thirty-one years in the early 1900s to sixty-seven at the end of the century.

CHAPTER FIVE

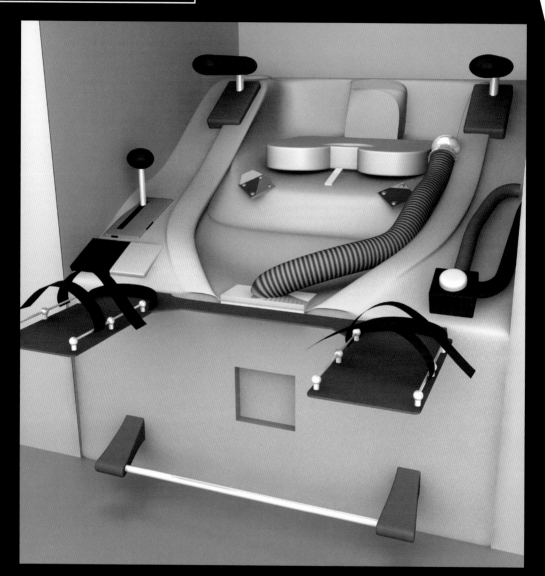

EVERYBODY LIVES DOWNSTREAM

> I do wish that I will get married in a family which has the facility of a toilet and separate water tap. It is a dream for me.
>
> —Barkha, twelve-year-old girl, Delhi, India, 2008

At the beginning of the twenty-first century, toilets finally made it into outer space when six research astronauts first began living on the International Space Station. The station is equipped with two Russian-built toilets, each valued at $19 million. Space toilets look like high-tech outhouses, and in a nod to tradition, one of the ISS toilets has a crescent moon design on its side like an old-fashioned American outhouse.

Orbiting Earth in a state of near weightlessness, crew members face unique challenges using the toilet. Without restraints, crew members float in the ISS, so to use the toilet, they must strap themselves to the toilet seat. They urinate into a long tube that resembles a vacuum cleaner hose. A funnel on one end of the tube adapts to male or female anatomy so that both men and women can use it. The fecal matter is stored on board and eventually disposed of back on Earth, while an onboard water recovery system recycles urine into drinkable water.

SPACE DUMP

In the earliest spaceflights, in the 1960s, astronauts released urine from spacecraft toilets into space. American astronaut Rusty Schweickart described the experience after his flight on board *Apollo 9* in 1969. "One of the most beautiful sights [in orbit] is a urine dump at sunset, because as the stuff comes out and as it hits the exit nozzle it instantly flashes into ten million little ice crystals."

Facing page: *This computer-generated illustration shows a toilet on the International Space Station. Users urinate into the long tube. Solid waste is freeze-dried for disposal back on Earth. The leg straps keep users in zero gravity from floating off the toilet.*

HIGH AND LOW

Back on Earth, toilet manufacturers such as the Japanese company Toto continue to develop high-tech toilet gadgets. Improvements include nozzles that clean the user's bottom with a spray of warm water and toilets that flush with recycled gray water (dirty water from sinks). Some high-tech toilets cost several thousand dollars. But while most people in the United States and other wealthy countries enjoy clean, comfortable indoor toilets, 2.4 billion people on Earth (that's four in ten global citizens) lack access to flush toilets and connections to public sewer systems. They dispose of their bodily wastes in open water, smelly pits, buckets, and even in plastic bags.

One sanitation specialist estimates that people without sanitary toilet options drink, eat, or otherwise take in—from their shoes, fingers, clothes, or insects that land on their skin or food—about one-third of

an ounce (10 grams) of fecal matter a day. Even one-tenth that amount can carry fifty diseases, one hundred worm eggs, one thousand types of parasites (such as the crypto that hit Milwaukee), and one million bacteria. The result of fecal contamination in humans is often diarrhea. In the United States, getting "the runs" is usually just an unpleasant annoyance. But in poor countries, diarrhea kills 2.2 million people a year.

This high-tech toilet from Japan's Toto company has a built-in seat heater, a volume-control knob for the flushing sound, and other gadgetry.

That's more deaths than are caused each year by either acquired immunodeficiency syndrome (AIDS), tuberculosis, or malaria. Children are especially at risk. In fact, every day, four thousand children around the globe die from diarrhea.

TRAIN TRACKS AND FLYING TOILETS

In India only 51 percent of households have a toilet of any kind. In fact, more people in India (53 percent) have cell phones than adequate sanitation. Indians without toilets defecate in fields, in streets, and along train tracks, which have been called the largest open toilet in the world. Indian journalist Chander Suta Dogra reports that her view from the train window always includes "scores of bare bottoms doing what they must."

Hanging toilets are a common feature of urban slums everywhere. Users pay a small fee to enter these makeshift, flimsy structures, which

A woman uses seawater to clean a hanging toilet in Petit Goave, Haiti. In poor nations, people build toilets from whatever they can find, such as the old sheets of metal in this structure.

hang over and allow waste to flow or drop directly into waterways. One such toilet is featured in a famous scene from *Slumdog Millionaire*, winner of the Oscar for Best Picture of 2008. Filmed in Mumbai, India, in slums where one million people live, the movie shows the main character falling from a hanging toilet into the swamp of human slop below.

Plastic bags do double duty as toilets in many parts of the world. Residents of Kibera—a slum in Nairobi, Kenya, and Africa's second-largest urban slum—refer to plastic bags as flying toilets. After defecating into them, they fling the bags as far as possible into the surrounding slum. Joseph Kisilu Muthiani lives in a small room in Kibera with his wife and four children. They have no toilet and usually can't afford the slum's pay toilets. In addition, Muthiani says, "It's not safe to go out at night as the toilets are far [away], so often we are forced to use polythene bags to relieve ourselves and dump them outside."

ALL AROUND THE TOWN

Open defecation isn't a problem only in poor countries. The 2010 US Census reveals that almost two million Americans lack the basic plumbing facilities that others take for granted. In US cities, homeless people must relieve themselves wherever they can. To call attention to the issue in Los Angeles, California, activist David Busch set up a makeshift toilet for the city's homeless population in 2012. He provided a bucket to squat on, toilet paper, soapy water, and towelettes inside a tent. Busch was arrested on charges of public nuisance. A Los Angeles court found him not guilty.

On the other side of the country, almost twenty years earlier, four homeless residents of New York City had sued the city to provide public toilets. Legal Action Center for the Homeless, which represented the plaintiffs, explained that without toilets the four were "forced to endure continual embarrassment, humiliation, physical injury and hazardous conditions." The center added that the lack of public toilets was a threat to public health: "New York is turning into a literal sewer. It's disgusting."

The homeless plaintiffs lost the case, but New Yorkers continued to rally for public toilets. Finally, in 2008 New York City installed the first of twenty planned public, self-cleaning, pay (twenty-five cents) toilets. The steel-and-glass stand-alone units are quite the space-age invention. After each use, the door automatically closes as the person exits, and a sweeping arm sprays disinfectant over the toilet and then blow-dries it. Jets propel disinfectant onto the floor.

A New Yorker enters one of the city's self-cleaning public pay toilets. Not only New York but also Paris, London, and some other big cities have this type of public toilet.

WORLD TOILET DAY

In early 2013, Hollywood star Matt Damon used humor to draw attention to the global lack of sanitation. Through Water.org, a nonprofit aid organization he cofounded, Damon released a video announcing that he was going on strike "in protest of this global tragedy." He joked, "Until this issue is resolved, until everybody has access to clean water and sanitation—I will not go to the bathroom." He invited supporters of the cause to donate to Water.org, which works to provide people all over the world with clean water and sanitary toilets.

Damon's symbolic strike continued until that year's World Toilet Day, celebrated annually on November 19. Launched in 2001, the World Toilet Organization (WTO) sponsors this international day of action. This group aims to break the taboo against talking about private bodily functions and toilets and to raise awareness of the global sanitation crisis. *Time* magazine named WTO founder Jack Sim of Singapore a Hero of the Environment in 2008. When Sim gives slide presentations about WTO, he includes a photograph of a little boy squatting outdoors to relieve himself. "That's me," he shares with his audiences, "circa 1961."

American actor Matt Damon uses his celebrity status and humor to bring attention to the global sanitation crisis.

IMAGINE WHAT'S POSSIBLE

Installing more flush toilets around the world is not the solution to the global sanitary crisis, experts say. Even low-flow toilets use a lot of water over the course of a day, and clean drinking water is increasingly in short supply around the world. What's needed instead, many say, are alternatives to traditional flush toilets.

The global Reinvent the Toilet Challenge aims to encourage creative solutions to the sanitation crisis. Sponsored by the Bill and Melinda Gates Foundation since 2011, the program awards more than $3 million each year to spur the development of a next-generation toilet. Teams of inventors from all over the world compete to design a toilet that doesn't flush away drinkable water. Toilets considered for the prize must meet specific criteria. They must recover the natural energy in human waste and turn it into fuel or fertilizer. They must kill all disease-causing germs. They must fit in crowded urban slums, where space is limited. They must also be cheap and easy to install. That's a tall order, but teams have come up with amazing solutions.

The top teams win money to develop their toilets further. One winning design removes water from human waste with a hand-operated vacuum pump. The reclaimed water can be used for watering crops. The remaining solids are recycled into fuel or fertilizer. Another design is a solar toilet that uses sunlight to disinfect urine and feces. The sun's heat turns waste into a kind of charcoal called biochar. Burned as a fuel in homes, biochar is more efficient and less polluting than wood charcoal. It could help save Earth's dwindling woodlands by cutting down on wood-charcoal use. Farmers can also add biochar to their fields to fertilize the soil. None of the winning toilets have yet gone into mass production.

The flush toilet that evolved in the 1800s may have seen its day. "Imagine what's possible if we continue to collaborate, stimulate new investment in this sector, and apply our ingenuity in the years ahead," Bill Gates said. "Many of these innovations will not only revolutionize sanitation in the developing world but also help transform our dependence on traditional flush toilets in wealthy nations."

TO SQUAT OR NOT

In much of Asia and the Middle East, and even in some bathrooms in Europe, people do not sit on toilets. They squat over them. Some squat toilets are made of porcelain and flush with water. They rest on the floor just like sitting toilets. Others are nothing more than holes in the ground. Research shows that a squatting position has health benefits. It takes less effort to evacuate the bowels when squatting, so squatting helps prevent constipation, straining that causes hemorrhoids, and other bowel disorders.

WHAT WORKS

In rural India, many young people are inspired by the No Toilet, No Bride campaign. It was started by a rural woman who married into a home without a toilet. She had to use community toilets (full of germs) or squat in fields (full of snakes). Women in India also risk rape when they relieve themselves in the open. The Indian government sponsors the No Toilet, No Bride program, which encourages women not to marry unless the groom's home has a bathroom. The radio advertising campaign includes jingles such as "No loo? No 'I do.'"

To address the problem of flying toilets in India and elsewhere, a company in Sweden developed sanitary bags called Peepoos. People urinate and defecate in the bags, which have a chemical lining to kill germs and reduce odors. Peepoos are biodegradable (they break down without hurting the environment) and also create economic opportunities. In the Kibera slum, for example, some residents operate Peepoo businesses, selling the bags and giving out partial refunds when users return filled bags. The waste becomes fertilizer.

Idda Andiwo, a Kibera mother of ten, used to rely on the slum's public pay toilets, which were expensive and dirty. Then she learned about Peepoo. "Since then," Andiwo said, "my five youngest children and I use it. It's a home toilet, which I use whenever, wherever. I also like the fact that it's single-use. Therefore I do not have to share it with anyone. So there's no fear of contracting diseases that are caused due to bad sanitation."

This toilet in Tiruchirappalli, India, was built specifically for children. The facility gives children a safe and clean alternative to open defecation or to using community latrines with adults. It includes child-sized toilets, plus a water tub and soap for washing up. Kids bring their own wash pans.

BACK TO NATURE

In the United States, a growing number of people are turning to an ancient practice: instead of flush toilets, they use toilets that compost excrement. These toilets allow waste to decompose naturally for later use as fertilizer.

Manufacturers make many different models of composting toilets, but they all work on the same principles. In a composting toilet, waste drops directly into a bucket or other container without the use of flush water. Materials such as sawdust or dry leaves absorb the moisture and reduce odors. Some composting toilets separate urine from feces. Organisms such as bacteria or earthworms then break down the waste. This process generates heat, though not enough to kill all the disease-causing germs in waste. These germs die naturally in about six months. The end product, sometimes called humanure, can be spread as plant fertilizer. Some homeowners use it on their gardens, but in some parts of the United States, laws forbid the use of humanure as fertilizer.

TP OVERLOAD

Americans spend $6 billion on toilet paper every year and use an average of fifty-seven paper squares per person per day. That adds up to 50 pounds (23 kg) of toilet paper per person per year. Multiplied by 318 million Americans, that's almost 16 billion pounds (7.26 billion kg) of toilet paper annually.

To reduce the environmental footprint associated with toilet paper usage, challenge yourself to use less toilet paper every day. This means less paper for sewage plants to process and fewer trees to meet the demand of toilet paper manufacturers. You can even try environmentally friendly cloth wipes, available on the Internet, as an alternative. After use, wash them in hot soapy water and reuse them.

If designed and managed well, composting toilets protect the environment by saving millions of gallons of precious flushing water. Composting toilets also help the environment by keeping waste out of waterways.

Toilets matter to everyone. In the 1800s, it took months for cholera to travel across the ocean. In modern times, germs and disease travel around the world in a matter of hours. With rapid global transportation, sanitation is not just a local matter. In the past, a community that dumped its raw toilet waste into a river spread disease to nearby downstream communities. In the twenty-first century, everybody lives downstream.

SOURCE NOTES

5 Jamie Benidickson, *The Culture of Flushing: A Social and Legal History of Sewage* (Vancouver: University of British Columbia Press, 2007), xxii.

7 Deut. 23:12–13 (New American Bible).

10 Jerome Carcopino, *Daily Life in Ancient Rome: The People and the City at the Height of the Empire* (New Haven, CT: Yale University Press, 1941), Google Books, accessed October 2, 2013, http://books.google.com/books?id=4lUVAAAAIAAJ.

10 Sextus Julius Frontinus, *The Two Books on the Water Supply of the City of Rome,* Google Books, accessed October 1, 2013, http://books.google.com/books?id=DkQ-AAAAYAAJ&q=270#v.

10 Michael Gilleland, "Sponge on a Stick," *Laudator Temporis Acti*, September 17, 2006, accessed September 26, 2013, http://laudatortemporisacti.blogspot.com/2006/09/sponge-on-stick.html.

13 Richard Smyth, *Bum Fodder: An Absorbing History of Toilet Paper* (London: Souvenir Press, 2012), Google Books, accessed October 2, 2013, http://books.google.com/books?isbn=0285641204.

13 Ibid.

14 British History Online, University of London and History of Parliament Trust, 2013, accessed September 26, 2103, http://www.british-history.ac.uk/report.aspx?compid=35973.

14 Ibid., http://www.british-history.ac.uk/report.aspx?compid=35972.

17 William Ian Miller, *The Anatomy of Disgust* (Cambridge, MA: Harvard University Press, 1997), 153.

17 Kathleen Brown, *Foul Bodies: Cleanliness in Early America* (New Haven, CT: Yale University Press, 2011), 37.

19–20 Ibid., 62.

21 Ibid., 124.

22 Ibid., 176.

22 Ibid.

22 Ibid., 162.

22 Martin V. Melosi, *The Sanitary City: Urban Infrastructure in America from Colonial Times to the Present* (Baltimore: Johns Hopkins University Press, 2000), 30.

22 Ronald S. Barlow, *The Vanishing American Outhouse: A History of Country Plumbing* (New York: Viking, 2000), ii.

23 "Classic Literature," *About.com*, accessed October 3, 2013, http://classiclit.about.com/library/bl-etexts/jausten/bl-jausten-em1-12.htm.

25 Dona Schneider and David E. Lilienfeld, *Public Health: The Development of a Discipline*, vol. 1 (Piscataway, NJ: Rutgers University Press, 2008), 257.

27 Roy Porter, *London: A Social History* (Cambridge, MA: Harvard University Press, 1998), 259.

27 Charles E. Rosenberg, *The Cholera Years: The United States in 1832, 1849, and 1866* (Chicago: University of Chicago Press, 1987), 3.

27–28 Ibid.

29 Charles Dickens, "American Notes for General Circulation," *Electronic Classics Series*, 2007, accessed October 4, 2013, http://www2.hn.psu.edu/faculty/jmanis/dickens/AmericanNotes6x9.pdf.

29 UCLA School of Public Health, "Writings of John Snow: The Cholera Near Golden-Square," accessed October 2, 2013, http://www.ph.ucla.edu/epi/snow/choleraneargoldensquare.html.

29 Ibid.

30 Mark Eaton Byrnes, *James K. Polk: A Biographical Companion* (Santa Barbara, CA: ABC-CLIO, 2001), 182.

30 Melosi, *Sanitary City*, 53.

31 Deborah Cadbury, *Dreams of Iron and Steel: Seven Wonders of the Modern Age, from the Building of the London Sewers to the Panama Canal* (New York: HarperCollins, 2004), 138.

31 Lemuel Shattuck, Nathaniel P. Banks Jr., and Jehiel Abbott, *Report of the Sanitary Commission of Massachusetts 1850* (Boston: Dutton & Wentworth, 1850), 196, Delta Omega, accessed October 2, 2013, http://www.deltaomega.org/documents/shattuck.pdf.

32 Ibid., 78.

32 "The Streets and the Cholera Again," *Chicago Daily Tribune*, July 12, 1854, 2, accessed September 29, 2013, http://www.nike-of-samothrace.net/csc.html.

32–33 Melosi, *Sanitary City*, 47.

35 "Quotes for Ed Norton," *IMDb*, 2014, accessed January 23, 2014, http://www.imdb.com/character/ch0023291/quotes.

36 Barlow, *Vanishing American Outhouse*, 4.

39 "Interview with Anna Novak," *American Life Histories: Manuscripts from the Federal Writers' Project 1936–1940*, accessed October 1, 2013, http://lcweb2.loc.gov/cgi-bin/query/D?wpa:31:./temp/~ammem_Cf3K.

42 "Bus-Sized 'Fatberg' Removed from London Sewer," *BBC*, August 6, 2013, accessed October 2, 2013, http://www.bbc.co.uk/news/uk-23584833.

45 "International Year of Sanitation Factsheet," *UN-Water*, 2008, accessed September 30, 2013, http://esa.un.org/iys/docs/5%20fact-sheet_achievable.pdf.

45 "There Ain't No Graceful Way: Urination and Defecation in Zero-G, Astronaut Russell Schweickart talking to Peter Warshall," *Space World*, January 1979, 16–19, National Space Society, accessed October 4, 2013, http://www.nss.org/settlement/nasa/CoEvolutionBook/SPACE.HTML.

47 Chand Suta Dogra, "Whole Lota Love," *Outlook India*, July 24, 2006, accessed October 3, 2013, http://www.outlookindia.com/article.aspx?231979.

48 "In Pictures: Flying Toilets," *BBC News*, 2009, accessed October 3, 2013, http://news.bbc.co.uk/2/shared/spl/hi/picture_gallery/07/africa_flying_toilets/html/2.stm.

48 Felicia R. Lee, "The Homeless Sue for Toilets in New York," *New York Times*, November 1, 1990, accessed October 5, 2013, http://www.nytimes.com/1990/11/01/nyregion/the-homeless-sue-for-toilets-in-new-york.html.

50 Matt Damon, "Strike with Me," *Water.org*, 2013, accessed October 5, 2013, http://strikewithme.org.

50 "Innovators for the Public: Jack Sim," *Ashoka*, 2007, accessed October 5, 2013, https://www.ashoka.org/fellow/jack-sim.

51 "Bill Gates Names Winners of the Reinvent the Toilet Challenge," Gates Foundation, 2013, accessed October 5, 2013, http://www.gatesfoundation.org/media-center/press-releases/2012/08/bill-gates-names-winners-of-the-reinvent-the-toilet-challenge.

52 Emily Wax, "In India, More Women Demand Toilets before Marriage," *Washington Post Foreign Service*, October 12, 2009, accessed October 5, 2013, http://www.washingtonpost.com/wp-dyn/content/article/2009/10/11/AR2009101101934.html.

52–53 "Idda Andiwo, Peepoo Customer," Peepoople, accessed October 3, 2013, http://www.peepoople.com/we-are-all-peepoople/urban-slums.

SELECTED BIBLIOGRAPHY

Ackroyd, Peter. *London Under: The Secret History beneath the Streets*. New York: Nan A. Talese, 2011.

Barclay, Eliza. "For Best Toilet Health: Squat or Sit?" *Shots: Health News from NPR*, September 28, 2012. Accessed February 23, 2014. http://www.npr.org/blogs/health/2012/09/20/161501413/for -best-toilet-health-squat-or-sit.

Barlow, Ronald S. *The Vanishing American Outhouse: A History of Country Plumbing*. New York: Viking, 2000.

Benidickson, Jamie. *The Culture of Flushing: A Social and Legal History of Sewage*. Vancouver: University of British Columbia Press, 2007.

Brown, Kathleen. *Foul Bodies: Cleanliness in Early America*. New Haven, CT: Yale University Press, 2011.

Carcopino, Jerome. *Daily Life in Ancient Rome: The People and the City at the Height of the Empire*. New Haven, CT: Yale University Press, 1941. Google Books. Accessed February 23, 2014. http://books.google.com/books?id=4lUVAAAAIAAJ.

Chadwick, Edwin. *Report on the Sanitary Condition of the Labouring Population of Great Britain*. London: Delta Omega Honorary Society in Public Health, 1842.

Frontinus, Sextus Julius. *On the Water-Management of the City of Rome*. Translated by R. H. Rogers. New York: Cambridge University Press, 2009. Accessed February 23, 2014. http://www.uvm .edu/~rrodgers/Frontinus.html#fn126.

George, Rose. *The Big Necessity: The Unmentionable World of Human Waste and Why It Matters*. New York: Metropolitan Books, 2008.

Gibson, Lydialyle. "The Human Equation." *University of Chicago Magazine*, May/June 2007. Accessed February 23, 2014. http://magazine.uchicago.edu/0726/features/human.shtml.

Jørgensen, Dolly. "The Metamorphosis of Ajax, Jakes, and Early Modern Urban Sanitation." *Early English Studies* 3 (2010): 1–31. Accessed February 23, 2014. http://dolly.jorgensenweb.net/files /Jorgensen-Metamorphosis_of_ajax.pdf.

Melosi, Martin V. *The Sanitary City: Urban Infrastructure in America from Colonial Times to the Present*. Baltimore: Johns Hopkins University Press, 2000.

Metcalfe, John. "What Really Happens after You Flush the Toilet." *Atlantic Cities*, July 3, 2012. Accessed February 23, 2014. http://www.theatlanticcities.com/technology/2012/07/what-really -happens-after-you-flush/2440.

Morgan, Peter. *Toilets That Make Compost*. Stockholm: Stockholm Environment Institute, 2006. Accessed April 11, 2014. http://www.ecosanres.org/pdf_files/ESR-factsheet-13.pdf.

Oleson, John Peter. *Oxford Handbook of Engineering and Technology in the Classical World*. New York: Oxford University Press, 2009.

Olmert, Michael. *Kitchens, Smokehouses, and Privies: Outbuildings and the Architecture of Eighteenth-Century Mid-Atlantic*. Ithaca, NY: Cornell University Press, 2009.

Porter, Roy. *London: A Social History*. Cambridge, MA: Harvard University Press, 1998.

Price, Catherine. "Humanure: The End of Sewage as We Know It?" *Guardian* (Manchester), May 12, 2009. Accessed February 23, 2014. http://www.theguardian.com/environment/2009/may/12 /humanure-composting-toilets.

Shattuck, Lemuel, Nathaniel P. Banks Jr., and Jehiel Abbott. *Report of the Sanitary Commission of Massachusetts 1850.* Boston: Dutton & Wentworth, 1850. Accessed February 23, 2014. http://www.deltaomega.org/documents/shattuck.pdf.

Snow, John. *On the Mode of Communication of Cholera.* London: John Churchill, 1855. Accessed February 23, 2014. http://www.ph.ucla.edu/epi/snow/snowbook.html.

Taylor, Craig. "The Disposal of Human Waste: A Comparison between Ancient Rome and Medieval London." *Past Imperfect* 11 (2005): 53–72. Accessed February 23, 2014. http://www.medievalists.net/2012/10/11/the-disposal-of-human-waste-a-comparison-between-ancient-rome-and-medieval-london.

World Health Organization. "Facts and Figures: Water, Sanitation and Hygiene Links to Health." 2004. Accessed February 23, 2014. http://www.who.int/water_sanitation_health/publications/factsfigures04/en.

———. "Global Burden of Disease: Part 2: Causes of Death." *World Health Organization*, 2004. Accessed February 23, 2014. http://www.who.int/healthinfo/global_burden_disease/GBD_report_2004update_part2.pdf.

Wright, Lawrence. *Clean and Decent: The Fascinating History of the Bathroom and the Water Closet.* New York: Viking Press, 1960.

FOR FURTHER INFORMATION

BOOKS

Albee, Sarah. *Poop Happened: A History of the World from the Bottom Up.* London: Walker Children's, 2010. This book answers questions about toilet technologies through the ages—from ancient Egypt to the modern space program.

Cadbury, Deborah. *Dreams of Iron and Steel: Seven Wonders of the Nineteenth Century, from the Building of the London Sewers to the Panama Canal.* New York: HarperCollins, 2004. This book includes a section on Joseph Bazalgette and the struggle to provide London with a sewer system.

Carter, W. Hodding. *Flushed: How the Plumber Saved Civilization.* New York: Atria Books, 2006. A fun read about water-delivery and sewage systems, this book moves from the plumbing of Rome to the sewers of London to the modern invention of the low-flush toilet.

Friedlander, Mark P., Jr. *Outbreak: Disease Detectives at Work.* Minneapolis: Twenty-First Century Books, 2009. This fascinating book for young adults examines a range of modern and historic epidemics and pandemics, including the plague of medieval Europe, to introduce readers to the investigative nature of epidemiological forensic science.

Johnson, Stephen. *Ghost Map: The Story of London's Most Terrifying Epidemic—and How It Changed Science, Cities, and the Modern World.* New York: Penguin, 2006. Part mystery, part history, all true, this book tells the story of how London's violent outbreak of cholera in 1854 spurred people like John Snow to solve the medical riddle of the age: How does disease spread?

Smyth, Richard. *Bum Fodder: An Absorbing History of Toilet Paper.* London: Souvenir Press, 2012. Just as the title promises, this is an amusing overview of the many things people have used as toilet paper throughout the ages.

Worsley, Lucy. *If Walls Could Talk: An Intimate History of the Home.* New York: Walker & Co., 2011. In this very readable social history of the bathroom, as well as the kitchen, the bedroom, and the living room, Worsley uses the history of the house to illustrate how people lived in earlier eras.

VIDEOS

George, Rose. "Rose George: Let's Talk Crap. Seriously." YouTube video, 14:02. Posted by TEDTalks. April 15, 2013. http://www.youtube.com/watch?v=ZmSF9gVz9pg. In this blunt, funny, and powerful talk, journalist Rose George discusses a once-unmentionable problem—the lack of basic sanitary facilities in many parts of the world. You can read more from George about this topic at http://rosegeorge.com/site/how-to-help.

"History of the Home: Bathroom." YouTube video, 14:56. Posted by edwardianpromenade. September 21, 2011. http://www.youtube.com/watch?v=inoVg5a1kps&feature=relmfu. This documentary relates the history of the bathroom and personal hygiene. Dr. Lucy Worsley, chief curator of Britain's Historic Royal Palaces, is an amusing guide to ever-changing attitudes about privacy, class, cleanliness, and technology. This link takes you to part 1. Be sure to watch all four parts.

"Overview: Metropolitan Council Environmental Services." YouTube video, 14:14. Posted by Metropolitan Council. December 21, 2010. http://www.youtube.com/watch?v=D1aABVbI4JE. In answer to the question What happens after you flush? this informative video shows how a sewage treatment plant works.

"The Poop Cycle." YouTube video, 3:12. Posted by ASAPScience. August 1, 2013. http://www.youtube.com/watch?v=hMIHFR_P7QY#at=165. ASAPScience's weekly videos cover the scientific aspects of everyday life—including toilets—in a simple and engaging way.

"The Scavengers: Can a Toilet Help Lift India's Untouchables out of Poverty?" YouTube video, 20:19. Posted by Journeyman Pictures. July 7, 2010. http://www.youtube.com/watch?v=mCecQrh8AZo. India's "untouchables"—a caste (group) of people at the bottom of India's social hierarchy—were traditionally expected to clean the toilets of all the other classes. This documentary describes Dr. B. Pathak's work to provide alternate jobs for them and to install basic public toilet facilities throughout India.

"Seven Wonders of the Industrial World: The Sewer King." Vimeo video, 48:32. Posted by Ramuel Tamayo. 2012. http://vimeo.com/20403418. Set in London during the 1850s, this episode of a British Broadcasting Corporation television series focuses on construction of the London sewerage system. The episode follows the efforts and work of engineer Joseph Bazalgette.

WEBSITES

Impatient Optimists: Water, Sanitation, and Hygiene
http://www.impatientoptimists.org/Topics/Water-Sanitation-Hygiene
This regularly updated site posts articles and photos about efforts by the Bill and Melinda Gates Foundation to improve toilets and sanitation around the world.

John Snow: A Historical Giant
http://www.ph.ucla.edu/epi/snow.html
This site from the University of California at Los Angeles School of Public Health is devoted to the life and times of public health legend John Snow (1813–1858).

Public Health Classics
http://www.deltaomega.org/classics.cfm
This site provides books and articles by pioneers in the field of public health. The classic works include *On the Mode of Communication of Cholera* by John Snow and the *Report of the Sanitary Commission of Massachusetts 1850* by Lemuel Shattuck.

Top 10 Famous Toilets
http://www.time.com/time/specials/packages/completelist/0,29569,2016258,00.html
This annotated slide show from *Time* magazine offers an array of famous toilets, including NASA's space toilet and "the most important toilet in art history" (Marcel Duchamp's 1917 urinal sculpture *Fountain*).

Toto
http://www.totousa.com
At this website, you can see high-tech toilets from the world's largest toilet manufacturer. One model is the washlet toilet, which provides a warm spray of water to wash the user's behind.

The Water Closet
http://theplumbingmuseum.blogspot.com
This blog from the Plumbing Museum in Watertown, Massachusetts, has a variety of articles about modern toilets, plus links to the museum's home site, where you'll find information about and photos of antique toilets and other plumbing artifacts.

Water.org
This site offers informative posts, videos, and photos about the lack of clean water, toilets, and sanitation around the world and presents many possible solutions. Water.org was cofounded by US actor Matt Damon.

World Toilet Organization
http://worldtoilet.org
Learn about World Toilet Day, hosted annually by the World Toilet Organization on November 19, and global efforts to provide sanitation to all people.

World Water Day
http://www.unwater.org/wwd08/flashindex.html
World Water Day, sponsored by the United Nations, focuses each year on a different aspect of water supply and use. This site has a wealth of sanitation information as well as an excellent gallery of photos from around the world.

Expand learning beyond the printed book. Download free, complementary educational resources for this book from our website, www.lerneresource.com.

INDEX

ABOUT THE AUTHOR

Francesca Davis DiPiazza is a writer and editor. Among her heroes are the people who keep the sewers running. Her books include *Friend Me! 600 Years of Social Networking in America* and *Zimbabwe in Pictures* (Visual Geography Series), both of which are Society of School Librarians International honor books. She lives and works in Minneapolis.

PHOTO ACKNOWLEDGMENTS

The images in this book are used with the permission of: © Ryan Cheng Photography/Flickr/Getty Images, p. 1 (background); © Glow Decor/Glow Images, p. 1; AP Photo/Ted S. Warren, pp. 4–5; Peter Langer / DanitaDelimont.com "Danita Delimont Photography"/Newscom, pp. 6–7; © Collection of the Lowe Art Museum, University of Miami/Museum purchase through funds from Mr. and Mrs. C. Ruxton/Love/ The Bridgeman Art Library, p. 8; © Joseph Calev/Shutterstock.com, p. 9; Dave Dunford/Wikimedia Commons, p. 12; © Bibliotheque Nationale, Paris, France/Archives Charmet/The Bridgeman Art Library, p. 15; © Private Collection/The Bridgeman Art Library, p. 16; Courtesy of the National Library of Medicine, p. 18; © The New York Historical Society/Archive Photos/Getty Images, p. 21; © Science and Society/SuperStock, p. 24; © National Maritime Museum, London, UK/The Bridgeman Art Library, pp. 26–27; The Granger Collection, New York, p. 28; Philadelphia Water Department/Wikimedia Commons, p. 31; © Lucinda Lambton/Arcaid/CORBIS, p. 33; © Frank Boellmann/E+/Getty Images, p. 34; Library of Congress LC-USZ62-77716, p. 37; © Chronicle/Alamy, p. 38; Library of Congress LC-USZC2-1594, p. 39; © David Sucsy/E+/Getty Images, p. 40; Qualit-E/Wikimedia Commons, p. 43; © Paul Wootton/Science Source, p. 44; © Marka/SuperStock, p. 46; Florian Kopp Image Broker/Newscom, p. 47; © NY Daily News via Getty Images, p. 49; AP Photo/Todd Williamson/Invision for Water.org, p. 50; © Saskia Castelein/WSSCC, p. 53.

Front cover: © Lucinda Lambton/Arcaid/CORBIS.
Back cover: © iStockphoto.com/LuisPortugal; © Lucinda Lambton/Arcaid/CORBIS (background).